HOPES, DREAMS
and WINGS

Tina (1964-2008), our daughter, was a born rebel. Since childhood she never bound herself to the routine set by us, rather did not allow it to be set. Notwithstanding this, she was a lovely and brilliant child who cared for the world in her own special way. She had a mind of her own and developed her personality as per her own convictions. She was a vibrant and vivacious person blessed with eyes full of life and a smile replete with mischief. While her jokes sent people into splits, she sat poker faced enjoying the fact that she had made others laugh. Her happiness was so obvious and yet so illusive that none of us ever realized her loneliness and associated pain. She was a girl who sold her joys to buy others' grief.

She was qualitatively different and made us wonder not so much because of her flamboyance but because of her unique intellect and style. Professionally qualified as a fashion designer in the early eighties, her designs were in great demand in the foreign markets and she herself was the model for her own creations.

Tina had hopes, dreams and the calibre to provide wings to her desire to scale the soaring heights she had set for herself. But God willed otherwise and recalled her to His abode, probably to assign her to another role befitting her magnificence.

We miss Tina's presence around us by the breath we take and have made this effort to bring our daughter alive by the medium of an anthology of her writings. We seek readers' blessings for our beloved daughter.

> Don't allow your wounds
> to transform you into
> something you are not.
>
> **Paulho Coelho**

HOPES, DREAMS and WINGS

Tina Khamesra

Presented by
Rajni Khamesra

Sterling Paperbacks

STERLING PAPERBACKS
An imprint of
Sterling Publishers (P) Ltd.
A-59, Okhla Industrial Area, Phase-II, New Delhi-110020.
Tel: 26387070, 26386209; Fax: 91-11-26383788
E-mail: mail@sterlingpublishers.com
www.sterlingpublishers.com

Hopes, Dreams and Wings
© 2011, Rajni Khamesra
ISBN 978 81 207 6036 3

All rights are reserved.
No part of this publication may be reproduced, stored in a retrieval system or transmitted, in any form or by any means, mechanical, photocopying, recording or otherwise, without prior written permission of the author.

Printed in India

Printed and Published by Sterling Publishers Pvt. Ltd., New Delhi-110 020.

Foreword

A very dear relation, a cousin sister who had lost her daughter a few years ago had come over to see me. She was carefully holding in her hand a pack of loose papers, placed carefully in light blue cover.

My sister softly spoke, 'I never knew Tina has been writing all this, looks like poetry'. She kept the pack on my table and said, "please go through it and tell me what these poems are all about?"

After late dinner, I carried the blue pack, and shuffled through the hand-written papers, rather casually. Gradually I began feeling that every passage was intense, direct, frank and personal than a poem would be.

I continued going through it, I don't know for how long. I felt I was neither sleeping nor I was awake. I felt I was afloat on a bed of ripples, at one moment moving in gentle, placid, rhythmic movements and all of a sudden transforming into mighty, fearful and devastating waves, bent upon pushing the shore line to the horizon and then disappearing with a loud thud in to deep darkness.

This is a collection of sounds and colours of hope, joy, laughter, pain, tearing-cry and despair of soul of a young woman trapped in a body of flesh and blood. It is memorable, touching, spontaneous and worth experiencing.

28/02/2011

Ved Vyas
Educationist and Former Principal
Modern School
Vasant Vihar, New Delhi.

Hopes, Dreams and Wings

When I went through Tina's work, I felt that she has observed almost all the phases of one's life with lot of precision. Her poetry is a detailed commentary which explains one's feelings, thoughts and emotions binding different stages of our journey on this planet Earth.

I feel that *Hopes, Dreams and Wings* is not only about Tina but about different experiences that life offers in respective ages. Almost all of us would be able to see some of our glimpses in her poems. The innocence of childhood, the exciting confusion in adolescence, the baffling choices in youth, the tug off between our aspirations and achievements, the mystery of life and death, the feeling of falling and rising in love, the feeling of being loved or betrayed, the feeling of caring and being cared for, the feeling of being together or alone. Tina talks about these feelings, in her poems and illustrates them the best in – "Adolescence, Empty Pocket and Tear Drop."

We all wish to rewind and review our lives to reflect back on ourselves. We all love to understand and acknowledge our experiences and emotions behind different scenes in our life drama. This anthology is an opportunity for all of us to do that.

Sweta Chaudhary
Clinical Psychologist

Tina's Life

I was going through most traumatic and agonizing period of my life. Our daughter Tina, our only child left for her eternal journey after a freak fall in a temple, it proved to be a final call from the God's domain.

It took me almost a year to realize that her house and the cats she had brought from the U.S. and lovingly called them her babies, needed my attention. Painfull but nevertheless necessary, I had to go through the arduous task of sorting out her personal belongings. While going through her stock of books I found three diaries carefully wrapped and I wondered what it was all about as I had never seen her writing even in earlier years.

When I opened the first diary and flipped through the pages, I realized how little I knew about my daughter's other side of personality. Tears welled up, then started flowing and as I read the contents of the first diary, realization dawned that there was a sheer volcano of pain hidden inside her. The very first page consisted of her inner turmoil—she had written.

"I guess the essence of true writing is pain, a high depression to be precise". Sometimes one wants to be away from one's own friends and relatives, however close they may be, though it is a terrifying experience many a times but necessary. Yes, I am lonely."

I went numb inside – how was it possible, Tina and lonely? She was such a vivacious, full of life with free laughter, hard core party lover since early eighties, with engaging, wide eyed, winsome innocent smile. She had mystical quality about her which attracted people immediately towards her and whoever she met almost got mesmerized by her personality and this quality made her immensely popular within her circle of her friends, cousins—who affectionately nicknamed her Tina – the CAT. She made every one dance to her tune and thoughts.

Since childhood she never bound herself to any discipline laid upon her, rather she didn't allow it. She was a born rebel and I knew, I had given birth to a daughter who was a lovely child with a mind of her own and developed her personality as per her own convictions. Vivacious, vibrant and bubbling with life, Tina had a mischievous smile and enjoyed when others laughed at her jokes cracked poker-faced, but it was all illusive.

She was qualitatively different and made us wonder not so much because of her flamboyant ways but because of her unique style, In those days, (early eighties), the type of her style was not accepted with openness as is now, must have proved a tough challenge and must have stifled her but she loved challenges and faced them bravely. She must have suffered in total isolation, that is why no one, even me, a Mother could realise her loneliness.

She had hopes, great dreams in her soulful lovely eyes to become one of the top fashion designers. One of the top designers of today who was also coming up a big name in those years remarked, " Tina, you must join me and you will be a big name in this industry," but she declined as she wanted to spread her own wings and reach the soaring sky. Once I commented critically on her design what she was wearing---in her typical flamboyant manner she said, "Come on Ma, one day after 15 or 20 years every girl, model or film star will be wearing these." How right she was. When I see today's film stars, models and even college girls--- I see Tina's face smiling and winking at me, "Hi Mom, what did I tell you"? "Yes my darling daughter you were right."

What saddens me is that all her hopes and dreams have got shattered. She spread her wings to reach the soaring heights, but the divine cut short her soulful journey.

As a mother I am paying my debt to her memory by publishing her original work. I leave it to the judgement of the readers what they think of this – poetry or an emotional soulful outcry of Tina.

Rajni Khamesra

Acknowledgements

I express my gratitude to God and thank Him for giving me strength, support and love which has enabled me to compile my daughter Tina's writings in the form of this book.

I thank my husband, Mahendra who has always been by my side in all my endeavors.

This book has seen the light of the day and I have to specially thank Ms. Rama Dhawan who is the force behind it and who inspired me to take up this initiative.

I am also grateful indeed to Ms. Shobha Pathan who extensively analysed Tina's collection and supported me in this endeavour.

Rakesh Malik deserves special thanks and gratitude who in spite of his tight schedule constantly extended his support at every step in this venture.

Ms. Romilla Bhagat, who has been a constant spiritual companion and a dear friend, who was with Tina during her last few hours on this earth saying spiritual prayers and providing her strength.

I am also blessed with some special friends who have just entered our lives a little while ago but their immense contribution plays a vital role in framing this work.

Amandeep, a budding Urdu poet has been an emotional anchor and has played pivotal role. She was instantaneously convinced that the collection must be published so as to make Tina come alive again.

Sweta Chaudhary, the very first person to bring the entire work in an order and spent a couple of sleepless nights, hammering the laptop. I cannot thank her enough for understanding Tina's entire collection of poems with precise perception.

Anuradha Goel, without who's coordianation Tina's work would not have been complete.

My thanks to Ved Vyas Bhai Sahib for giving a foreword to this anthology.

Thanks are also due to Col Vinod Awasthy, Sena Medal, Anuj Dhawan and Shantanu Awasthy for their invaulable love and affection, who have taken time off their busy schedule to remember Tina as they knew her.

My affectionate thanks to Sudha Dhawan, Smiriti, Nutan Kumar and Shibani Bhojwani and Jaya (my sisters and nieces).

Last but not the least I thank Sterling Publishers Pvt. Ltd., to have provided me this beautiful medium to have Tins's collection of thoughts to put across to poetry lovers. I express my special thanks to Mr. S.K. Ghai for this understanding my emotional self and agreed to publish this book.

My thanks to Cheena who always welcomed me with a cheerful smile, Sudipto, Harish Bhardwaj and above all—the positive vibes which emanated from the premises of Sterlings.

Contents

Foreword	5
Hopes, Dreams and Wings	6
Tina's Life	7
Acknowledgements	9
It is called Adolescence	15
Zindagi	17
Empty Pockets	17
Love	17
Petal	18
Oasis	18
Pain	18
Alone	19
Mixed Veg	20
Evening	21
Tie Bond	21
Waiting	22
Anticipation	22
Wonder	23
A Day without You	23
Ties	23
Paint Box	24
Pain	24
Pearls of Memories	25

Yours	25
Wilderness	25
Love Was	26
State	26
Why and How?	26
Sound	27
A moment in time	27
You left	27
Paperback	28
Gone	28
When you left	28
Brainwash I	29
Brainwash II	29
You say you care	29
Stream of Hope	30
You and Them	30
You	30
Beautiful life	31
Life and Time	31
Promises	32
Skeptic	32
Happiness and Tears	32
Helpless	33
Loneliness	33
Lost	33
Longing	34
Pardon	34

Who knows?	35
Dead End	35
Togetherness	36
Betrayal	36
Rainfall	36
Past	37
Gone/forever	37
Tear Drop	37
I am an Artist	38
Motto	38
Sail to Escape	39
Ode to Doubts	39
Findings	40
Contradictions	40
Now	40
It Shines	41
Swan I	41
Swan II	42
Swan III	42
Dry Eyes	42
The Pain	43
Now or Never	43
Burnt Pages	44
Club	44
I Don't Know	45
True Tears of Joy	45
I am	45

Evening is high	46
Gone	46
My battle	47
That's All	47
Love	47
Again	48
Fallen and still Falling	49
I wonder	49
Road across	50
Mirage	50
Fate/Destiny	51
Karma	51
Dusty the Cat	51
Life and Destiny	52
Love and Death	53
Death	53
Soaring high	54

Remembering Tina

Tina and I	57
Tina my Sister	59
Fondly Always	61

It is called Adolescence

It is the age when one climbs and falls, Learns and crawls,
It is the time of fifteen to eighteen, of memorable dreams, of apprehensions and waitings,
When the heart learns to skip a beat, and flames brighten by the ignited heat.
It is when one shies or one embarrasses,
When one holds imaginary conversations, believing innocently with eyes full of anticipations,
It is awkward to be an adolescent, and more so behaving like decent,
One doesn't know what one wants; one doesn't know what the limit is,
The life is confined to a limited bond, not knowing the openness of the freedom,
It is when one dotes endlessly on beloved; it is when one loves all and hates none,
It is when one is misunderstood, when one is burdened with the authentic and shameful facts of life,
Of the do's and don'ts of the meagre allowances
It is when one wants to outgrow these frocks and bloomers, to spring into the tights,
Imagine the breeze and fragrance on the faces, love the moon and think with awe and fear,

It is forced on one unexpected and unwanted, it doesn't really matter whether one's life gets abated,

It is when one strives hard to impress and to please, to exaggerate and never cease,

It is the time of dwelling into dreamland of springs and pearls, dews and grass,

There is uncertainty and doubt, the mind drowns into the depth of thoughts and ambitions,

Lacklustered inspirations; it is a delicate carnation,

Sweet and charming, yearning to be cherished and nurtured.

It is adolescence!

Zindagi

Zindagi bhi cigarette ki tarah hoti hai
Enjoy karo,
Warna sulag to rahi hi hai,
Khatam to waise bhi ho jayegi!

Empty Pockets

Time for *bidis* and may be a quarter
Money in shortage
Abundance of empty pockets
Drawing from banks
Skeptical and apprehensive
Not knowing where the next penny will drop from

Love

Definition of love
Can never be defined
Only felt by two hearts
and emotion so gullible, so naïve
Only to be felt, never seen
Accept in the form of gestures
Known only to you and me

Petal

Life not ever being a bed of roses
When I'd wanna lie,
Yet a petal fell in my lap from somewhere
And I caressed my cheeks with it
So what if I can't rest my head on one?

Oasis

As it goes on and into yet for want of love
We all live in a world of illusion
But the movement and the move towards
The oasis remains dry,
After all it's only an illusion

Pain

Love, faith, trust and honesty,
Nothing known nothing gained,
All lost in a moment of time,
Washed away by a deluge of pain

Alone

I was alone,
I cried alone,
Laughed alone,
In this lonely world of hate, of malice,
No passion or compassion,
No companion, no friend,
No one to call my own
I cried out, my heart poured,
Through lonely nights, having painted their darkness
Into infinite heights where only two stars sparkled
And a streak shone,
But alas, they were also alone

I die, I live, I live and die
The vicious circle of life goes on,
I make my own wheels,
My own circles and my own race
I win this race because I am alone,
But what does it matter?
There is no other participant,
No one else to cheer,
So I cry out my victory to myself

I called to life
But she also was lonely like me
What reality makes the difference is
That I, with no anticipation, no apprehensions, no inhibitions
Lived her and she with them lived for me
Then I realized I had someone

Mixed Veg

Trapped in this world of veg,
I am a Potato
Sometimes twice baked, sometimes fried
May be raw and seasoned
Green & yellow
They stare back at me
So does the hen
Only the comb's missing
And the ox lost his tail long ago
One of them has a family called
Mr. & Mrs. Mixed Veg

Evening

I feel us, I feel you, I feel love, I feel sex
I feel so beautiful
I feel a dimple on my left check
And I feel my left shoulder where I feel my collar bone
And a whisp of hair tumbling from my crown
I feel the woman in me but
I listen to rock machine as I hear my tub filling
Tomorrow morning I will see an empty tank
Just the way I see my cheeks blushing right now
And feel the woman in me come alive
I'll make love tonight

Tie Bond

Never be sad, never be sorrowful
Forever lives my love for you,
This heart of mine blooms with fragrance
Of memories so sweet
So do you think I would break this bond?
So tight, between you and me?

Waiting

The day moves on
Dragging its feet across the road and through the woods
Beyond the tree talks
A few flocks of red and patches of green dark in light
A row of black wings highlight the setting sun
And I dread the night
When waiting becomes another part of life
I wait, I listen and I hear the sounds of darkness
When crickets chirp and the wind whistles
But the phone does not ring

Anticipation

When the love has flown and gone far away
Where do I fly after it?
Or, do I wait for it to slide down in a flight of never never?
Only to convince myself that it never was?

Wonder

When does sorrow begin and when does it end?
When life has just begun or when you are halfway through?
That's when you wonder as to what it was all about?
Was it worth it or just a matter of fact?
You are still fighting

A Day without You

A day in life
So lifeless and listless
Yet I carry on,
Knowing there is hope, for tomorrow
Will you be there?

Ties

Life in a turmoil and they talk about ties?
Ties untimely, un-gained?
For what and whom, we never will know
Where the end lies, with knots & ties?

Paint Box

Bright was the colour of my paint box
Bright was the colour of my life
Bright was the colour on my room wardrobe,
Till you entered
Now it's hurting and bruised and colourless
Why? Is my question, can you answer?

No, b'cause answer is so obvious
And consequences so bad
Yet I hang on to dream
So fetid and infected
With your indifference
That it has turned into a nightmare
I try to colour it with my paint box

Pain

Pain begets pain, when we drown
In an embrace of love and sing a lullaby
For our souls already silent
Only to awaken, ironically
a dead beginning.

Pearls of Memories

A rose flung in the air
And the petals scattered
Scattering over the lyrics of my heart
The dew shining on them
Were my tears,
The pearls of my memories

Yours

Too old to be your wife
Too young to be your mother
Only old enough to know you and be there
When you need me
Just when you fall
And I pick the debris you leave behind

Wilderness

The cancer of love has eaten the within of my heart
Empty and withdrawn, only the debris of what was
Which was a true heart that had loved once
Will a flower ever bloom in the wilderness of the ruins?
Or will some one come and dig the sapling out?

Love Was

Love was never meant to be only a phase in life
That's what all it will be,
Going and coming whenever I wish it to
Not knowing how I'll accept the inevitable
That is heart ache

State

The state to live or die
Is a state to be or not to be?
Whether to give or to take
Same as goes earlier,
Yet we fight for what?
Know not I, nor you

Why and How?

Once a life and then follows death
Then why & when, we do not know
And how, is yet to be deciphered
Which & what is difficult to comprehend,
Yet we try and move towards the inevitable

Sound

The sound of another voice
Is that me?
May be it is another's
Yet it could be mine
Breaking the sound of silence within
While the dim outside grows

A moment in time

A call, a change
A moment in time,
All it took to erase the memories from my mind
But yet I hung on to the inevitable
And for the dollar and dime

You left

You left me in an empty room
Filled with memories and a broken heart,
Loneliness but no knots
You just left me with pain and a chompy

Paperback

Flames of jealousy
Pain in the heart
Caused by love that was
No longer is mine
Burnt the past that could have been
A part of our future
In paperback

Gone

And then I saw my end so near
To be forgiven and forgotten
Over the years gone,
By gone and you were gone

When you left

When dawn arrives,
You will leave not to return may be,
Until the dusk follows
Till then I will die a slow death
Only to revive my senses
When I see your face again
Against the setting sun

Brainwash I

Washes out and gone is my mind,
Caught between time and circumstances,
Never to be the same again
Tomorrow only brings pain
Only if tomorrow comes

Brainwash II

So when time ran out,
I thought was it "to be or not to be"
Or was it "to be is not to be"
Mere existence, a general survival
And then when I moved on a never returning point

You say you care

You say you care, I hear nothing
You say you feel, I see nothing
You say you want, I get nothing
You believe you are there, I see nothing
The false lies that your actions prove
And I get carried away,
Yet to move by your side
Shoulder to shoulder, foot for foot

Stream of Hope

Forever and ever and time to come
I dreamt of a home, never to be,
Yet I carried on
In hope of time and space,
When one makes way for the other
The stream never stops flowing

You and Them

Pain creeps in, slow and pulsating and days pass
As I know you are one of them
Yet I hold on and keep to myself what is mine
Untouched by alien hands

You

The touch of your hand on my skin
So warm, rushes the blood through my stream
The warmth of your breath caressing my cheeks
Enhances my blush
The heartbeat I feel through mine, all yours
Makes me believe I belong to you

Beautiful life

When the window of my heart
Gently swayed open
And the gentle mist lingered over the woods
A tissue of cool breeze fluttered in
Ruffling my hair,
The golden rays filtering through the locks
I rose above it all
And loved you more
Each morning I woke up sad
Today I was not the same,
The world seemed beautiful
My heart soared and life seemed buoyant
And I loved you more.

Life and Time

So long so good was
Never to be otherwise
Till I fell in love
Then it was may be, may be not
And we all depended upon the inevitable.

Promises

Together promises are made
And a single heart breaks
When time runs against odds,
I shut, yet tear drops fall
And splashing drops wet my life
I drown in sorrow,
Survival seems minimal when living is inane

Skeptic

For what and when I travelled on
Yet not to know what life had in its lap
For me to rest or go on and there to withdraw
From those and whom I know not, I play on

Happiness and Tears

Happiness and tears seem to have become a paradox
And life has become mundane
Whether or not I need to move on
I wonder and wander,
Why I slip gradually
Down the ladder of destiny

Helpless

Time forwarded in my lap
And I engulfed it all
That's what it's meant to be
Little did I know where it would end
Or would it be the beginning of the end
Time and space had me suspended
Worse than a pendulum swinging in your direction

Loneliness

That little room
That little space
Where I had held and then
You walked in,
Yet I was alone
B'cause you weren't you
You were them

Lost

Forbidden and forgone was my love in life
Till I met you my heart, my love and my soul devoted,
Yet unaccepted by your suspicions
Led me to a path never ever

Longing

I waited for the speckled light to fall
I waited for it to become a streak
My waiting turned my heart bleed with yearning
My desire burnt all night and drown in the morning
Oh! The waves of the unfathomable sea,
Causing a turmoil, the ache beating hard
My mind throbbing, the tears flowing,
The alien speck lost into an alien darkness
Passing by quickly through a streak
But alas! It was utterly strange
Sigh! My waiting turned into an abyss of longing

Pardon

For now and in the least
While my heart bleeds and the wound still raw
I forgive thee your sins unforgivable
I deny myself that love I need
Only to cleanse your soul
Hence I punish myself

Who knows?

Explaining and demeaning
Went hand in hand
When I met you again
Only to confront the main and the non-fundamental
Those that don't matter, yet I carry on
With only one belief that it's you
Who will change some day some time

Only future knows apart from us
And left to be alone, no where
Yet I feel I belong and I stay to be
What I am
Only to know who I am and where I belong

Dead End

Missing you is not so easy as loving you
Yet I carry on and move towards
A never ending end
While the road shows nothing
But a dead end

Togetherness

Who cares for who?
Know not I, but I believe
Somewhere and sometime
There will be you and me
Forever to be

Betrayal

And then when I turned my back on you
It's hard to learn,
Just when I was about to live
You came and dug my grave

Rainfall

Tell me, is it raining? Raining out of blues?
Bright are skies of tomorrow
Opening for me and you?
It is time that living could not be so easy if you are on fire
My love will extinguish
Dreams of rainfall pitter patter on the pane
Like my tear drops falling when you are away

Past

And then the past
Glorified itself in the form of a face
Wrinkled and sedate
Lines of wisdom not age
And I relented to be where I don't belong

Gone/forever

Forever as years have gone by
And memories have haunted me,
Nightmares of reality seen authentic day by day
Moments of despair trail around my path of love
And I go round and round in vicious circles

Tear Drop

And today I thought of a bird in free flight high & happy,
Yet a drop of rain fell on me
Despite the skies being so clear
It was only a tear drop

I am an Artist

What is beauty to me, is abstraction to you
I feel it, you see the crudeness
I see delicacy, you see harshness
I see softness, you see blatantly
I see blindly

My world are the stars, clouds, sun, moon,
And petals,
But you know earth, rocks, bones and air
I sit on clouds and sing, you lie on bed and fling
I cry tears on the green grass
You trample the grassy dew
They are pearls to me, you flick them away
You know, you may
I imagine, I create, I am an artist

Motto

Enhancement of power
The lust for control
To dominate this con world and
To relieve by bonds of any ties

Sail to Escape

To lose somebody
To have loved the same
In an ocean of pain in which I sail
But the catamaran refuses to drown
And my oars and sails are affront

I know my end is nigh
B'cause the sands are close in sight
And I know that a fish net is waiting
Spreading on the wet salt
But this time I know how to escape
The ebbed ropes

Ode to Doubts

This tear drops
And ode to you forever
Yet you won't wipe it away
To clear my doubts and fear
What then are you there for?
Only then will I know
When the glowing embers of faith burn bright

Findings

Tentacles of doubt creep in and grip my faith and love
To be or not to be, in or out of the shell
Is all up to me yet not so for time will tell
And decipher, the difference between then and now

Contradictions

Roses bloom and fade away fast
In form of dried petals
Why do the cacti live longer?

A desert nurtures them and fertile soil the plants,
Yet fertility cannot prevail on a dried up land

Now

Repetitions and comprehensions are beyond we
What I know and comprehend is the end
The end of an era, an era so great
Now is the time to move on
And make what I broke
Yet time will tell when it is to be

It Shines

Life was but an un-penetrable hole
But I entered, it was dark
In there I could see it
Lie over turned
It was Alladin's lamp
Still which shone not within the hole
Not outside but all alone, inside me
My eyes sparkled, to make vision clear
But did I see anything?
No, I didn't because I was blind!

Swan I

A price I paid so heavy and dear over the times and years,
A swan that flew away only to shed tears
When the world held the reins and pulled the strings of life,
I held back and resisted
Because long ago I had flown away
I guess we all pay a price, once in a while
And a heavy one that too

Swan II

Life, I put at a stand by, just to wait and watch
Tired watching I whacked away
Never to return
When dawn arrived and I opened my eyes
It was too late
Because the reflection of the swan had faded away

Swan III

I spread my wings to soar again
But the winds held me back
I knew the time had come for me
To sit back and relax

Dry Eyes

When you cry and the tears don't fall
Only when the sob is stifled by the un-stinging dry eyes,
Shedding pain hopelessly,
The heart aches to a point
Until you go numb
And then nothing else
Matters any more

The Pain

She sat on the step thinking, feeling empty,
She didn't feel like crying at his having left her and gone
She felt a pain which distorted her expression
It was a pain which one feels
When an important one's body has been separated
And kept away in a preservatory for medical purpose,
The pain when a precious treasure one has cherished
All throughout life, ever since the childhood
Has been snatched away,
A pain one feels when one's finger has been pinched with a needle,
When one is feeling faint
That pain which comes from somewhere far away,
One feels the sting, but too nauseated and dizzy to bother,
Her pain was the same

Now or Never

Now or never
And whenever or whatever
Who knows, yet we all strive,
I will too probably towards a road leading to a dead end

Burnt Pages

Living by the means of end and remembering
The torn pages of my life and fate
Burning to ashes while I watch the flames
And burn my fingers trying to salvage what I can
I find my hands full of cinders
That burn through my soul till today
The burnt pages are nothing but debris of my past
Burnt and gone long back,
You destroyed my book

Club

Just a din of the music and waiting for a drink
While I watch the whole crowd and hear them screaming
Will we be the victims too or only spectators?

Here I sit and wonder,
What's wrong with life?
Yet I see what ought not to be, that is inside

Who is to blame who is to know,
When life comes to an end
Only then will I know where is the end,
It's for you and me to decide

I Don't Know

Strange yet so true, on that fateful day sigh when I met you,
I didn't know my world would fall apart,
And shatter my dreams so unreal
What seemed reality then
Was only an illusion, a mirage?
That faded just when I extended my heart towards you

True Tears of Joy

When did I see them last?
When did they trickle down my cheeks?
And form a pool of blood?
Know not I nor you,
Because you never cupped your palms,
Fearing they will overspill,
Alas, the tears of blood dried long back

I am

And then he spoke of me,
Yet I carried my self away from myself
Then what was the need to give me am
Imprisonment not for me
Just b'cause I am a woman?

Evening is high

Shades of blue, white & grey
And a duster of dots flying by,
A few green arms
Flapping their wings
And the breeze
Gently caressing my face,
Rustling through my tresses and telling me,
Evening is high,
Just then the moon winks at me
And tells me,
I am following soon!

Gone

Upside down and inside out and forward fast
Yet I know you are you and not mine
Despite moments spent in isolation
With each other
Yet the times spent and gone now
And all that is left
Is loneliness of its own kind
Between you and me

My battle

May fate, my misfortune make me smile
At the state I am in, yet I fight
But what for? Can you explain?
No it is my battle that I gotta fight, and win
If I can, I think I will

That's All

Will I live or die? Know not I
Will I be there? Who knows?
Only time is the witness to my whereabouts
And that's the end of my beginning,
That's all!

Love

Do I still believe in love?
Or is it only a fantasy?
Does it exist or only poetry?
Knowing, I remain incognizant

Yet I believe it will come
And then I will call it a day
When love does not remain
A question mark any more

Again

And a birth given and a death forgiven
Is not to be thrown or deciphered
It is the moment of forgiveness is accepted
For a life time

Life on its own is forgiving enough
To be by myself

Spring and summer passing by
These things let me drown,
Don't know why
Words and lyrics don't make life
Yet hold a meaning unknown
To you and me.

Yet we try to search for the inevitable
That just might not by laying in the pot of gold
At the end of the rainbow.

Running back to me and opening your arms wide open
and a paradox between being a friend and lover.

Fallen and still Falling

I receive a call of future
Knowing I can't hold on
Probably the end is near yet so far
That I can't touch it
If only I could
Then the end won't be an end any more
It will become present or may be future

I wonder

Daylight draws near
Yet a curtain of darkness engulfs my mind
Shadows of pain
Visible in the horizon
Cast the spell of loneliness
And I find myself treading the path of sorrow
I wonder if there ever will be a dawn of happiness,
   of hope:
Will the sun shine again to brighten my life?
Void of laugh and joy.

Road across

People coming, people going
On a road that I see the beginning
Not knowing where it leads to
Where it ends
Yet they come and go
Some day I will too
When the gates open
I will reach the destination
The unknown end.

Mirage

The spirit of life keeps me alive and going
A euphoric state like a bubble,
about to burst into fragments,
that only reflect pain.
Little do I realize what I have lost
in the shadows of sorrow,
like a few drops on an expanse of sandy deserts.
We all believe in Mirage.

Fate/Destiny

And life ended abruptly
Only just when it had begun
To lead me to a rainbow
But b'cause it took a wrong path
It followed to an end of disaster
An aim that I had left far behind
Into the hands of destiny/fate

Karma

Life moves on but time
is a tunnel.
Through which it travels,
I do not know the fateful destination.
But can predict my destiny,
And that is my karma.

Dusty the Cat

Dusty growls unpredictably
Just like life
Either bear the brunt of it
Or else growl back

Life and Destiny

Life is
like a flying bird, soaring across the skies
of a dream
Hoping to see the horizons
of desires and fulfilment.
When the time comes
and the moment is nigh
The bubble bursts
only for me to see bits
and pieces of a never, never,
The one I thought, was
a dream come true
Only to realize
that a dream is more
often a nightmare
Than hope turning
into reality.

Love and Death

Love and death are two uninvited guests,
When they will come no one knows,
But both do the same work,
One takes the heart
And the other takes its beats.

Death

They don't care till you survive
They don't care when you are dead
Only a few Ah's & Ooh's
And for them the pain subsides
But what about those who still mourn
For them will the Sun ever shine?

Soaring high

He held the Kite
and tugged the string.
It soared high
in a graceful flight.
But it was not paper
nor was the thread.
He held the kite of my life
He tugged the string of my heart
I whispered it was me
and not a kite
But still my soul,
my heart and my whole being
They soared up, higher and higher
In a mistful flight
But I felt lighter than a Kite

Remembering Tina

Tina and I

I do not recall the day I first met Tina, a niece to me from my wife's side of the family. I do, however, remember a plump little girl, very vibrant and very demanding in what she wanted or did not. I was a young Second Lieutenant those days and she started addressing me Lieutenant 'Thee' in her unique and very girlish style. As I grew in rank and service in the organisational hierarchy, she kept adding the current rank to the constant prefix 'Thee'. So, to Tina, I have been, over the years, Lieutenant Thee, Captain Thee, Major Thee and so on. It was not very often that I got to meet her during early days of my courtship with her aunt. But even during those brief meetings, I foresaw her future. I had no doubt that Tina will grow into a good looking, intelligent career woman with a mind and heart of her own. That she did, is, therefore, no surprise to me. But the fact that she achieved so much in so little a time, and then left for her heavenly abode is what has left me astonished.

Tina was an achiever with a burning desire to excel in whatever she did. During an early meeting of ours, after her aunt and I were married, I remember telling her that she was too fat for her age. It was a remark made in a lighter vein because she was only a teenager and the fat on her was nothing but the baby fat, all teenagers have. But Tina took the remark seriously and asked me as to when will I be on leave the next time. To my query as to why she asked the question, she stated, with the arrogance of a queen, "Come and see me then". Six months later when I met her again, I was in for a shock. That Tina had worked on herself was obvious. Gone was the little plump girl I had seen six months ago. Standing before me was a young stunning beauty with an hour glass figure and long flowing tresses, an epitome of a successful Indian model. While I stood admiring her, she seemed oblivious to the appreciation she was being showered upon by all around her.

Tina remained beautiful not only physically but also as a human being. She was exceptionally intelligent and singularly focused. Emotional and sensitive, she was also endowed with a great sense of humour. Tina and I shared an intimate relationship with my mother-in-law and Tina's grand-mother, one of the most beautiful and kind women I have met in life or will ever meet. Tina spent considerable time with the old lady during her last few years and was always playing jokes to keep her amused. She would often tease her about the number of children she had, had nine of them in all and will ensure that Biji apologised to her for having produced so many. One day while she was at it, the old lady stunned and amused Tina, stating, "Alright, it was a mistake; please forgive me, I would produce no more now".

The only chink in Tina's otherwise strong and incredible persona was her emotional debility. She easily trusted people and became dependent upon them with slight display of affection towards her. Had she been business like in her feelings towards fellow human beings, Tina would have been living a very successful life today. As I hold grudges against those who exploited this beautiful girl, I deeply regret her premature departure from this world which never gave her what was due to her for her brilliance. May God bless her soul.

A collection of Tina's poems written over the years, many of them while she was suffering loneliness, feeling deserted and unwanted. They are a true reflection of emotional upheavals and betrayals this young girl suffered during her short span of life. That she was in pain is obvious but that she suffered it alone without spreading dismay around her physical world was also obvious to those in her vicinity. Never did I find her, sans zest and an urge to enjoy every moment that she lived on this planet. That her emotional debility was exploited to the hilt by those who claimed to love her has been portrayed beautifully in these poetic gems. Understanding the sum and substance of these poems is not easy and will only dawn upon an intellectually endowed and emotionally surcharged reader. Happy reading!!

New Delhi　　　　　　　　**Colonel Vinod Awasthy, Sena Medal**
　　　　　　　　　　　　　　　　　　　　Indian Army

Tina my Sister

I was born an Army child and grew up enjoying the company of plenty of people at home; the orderlies, maids and their children. But none of them was a friend to me. I remember I often played with my pens and pencils all by myself and very rarely with my father who would throw his overwhelming military authority at me every time I failed to hit the ball the way he thought it should have been hit. Sooner than later, I became a loner and this peculiar personality trait got compounded as my parents decided to let me be their only child. I would have grown into a recluse had a vivacious girl named Tina not entered our household while I was barely four years old.

Tina was my first cousin and she came to visit my parents in that capacity while my father was posted at the National Defence Academy, Kharakwasla. She barged into my little cocoon and swept me out of it before I realized. The extrovert, people friendly and the outgoing person that I am today is because I have spent a great deal of time in Tina's company. She was my sister, friend and a confidant as long as she lived. I have always admired and learned from her unique ability to strike back when faced with adversities. It is often said that creativity is allowing yourself to make mistakes but art is knowing which ones to keep. Tina was never afraid of committing mistakes but she knew for sure which ones to keep. A naturally gifted girl who was way ahead of her times in every sense. I have vivid memories of her style, effervescence, exuberance and vivacity which forever made her a cynosure of all eyes. Family get-togethers and parties were incomplete and insipid without her rib tickling jokes. Tina always drew a lot of attention and had this unique ability to drop a word or phrase at the appropriate moment making the crowd crack out of their shells. What always worked for her was a combination of stunning looks and high intellect. She knew more about current affairs and the issues of the day than most. Because of her keen personal interest in all things, she was not great at hiding her surprise when I would tell her I did not know anything about something or the other! She expected all of us to be as interested in everything as she was, at times a tough act to follow. The funny thing is that I do not remember a day when I saw Tina reading a newspaper or listening to the news. My friends and family know that I always appreciated and admired Tina a great deal. I never hesitated to include her in my activities or gatherings, knowing fully well that she would probably be the most interesting person there. A testament to this was the wide variety of age groups and people she had as friends. Tina loved entertaining people and would often cook for them. I believe her love for cooking was an extension of her artistic gift. I cannot say that she was fond of cooking because she entered the kitchen only on select occasions but when she did, the results were finger licking. She set high standards for us with her well cooked and sumptuous food and more importantly, elegant hostessing skills.

Her most notable quality was her ability to stay loyal to whosoever she liked and loved. She even cared for people who wronged her. Probably, it is this quality of character that cast an evil shadow on Tina's vibrant personality and tore her apart from her zest for life.

She suffered a great deal loving people but not receiving the reciprocation that she deserved.

Tina is no longer with us in this physical world. But I still feel her vibrant presence around me and she still renders me a sane advice in a tricky situation as I think of what she would have done in a similar impasse.

I am certain Tina is in good company wherever she is, after all she always secured for herself nothing but best.

The book containing her poems written over the years is a mother-loves-tribute-to-her-only-child.

I am sanguine the reader will feel the emotion and the intellect with which Tina put these pearls to paper. Happy reading!!

Singapore   **Shantanu**

Fondly Always

I knew Tina my whole life – she was 2 years older so we virtually spent our growing years together; she was big sister and always got her way with me, and I simply doted on her. We were cousins (our mothers are sisters), but our bond transcended even a brother-sister relationship. We were best friends, we laughed together, played together, got into trouble together, fought like cats and dogs, yet we were inseparable. When Tina left us all, I felt like a piece of me had been ripped out and lost forever.

My earliest memory of Tina is from the 70's. We lived in Calcutta and Delhi was always the destination for summer holidays. Tina and I had no siblings, so we were drawn to each other – she had always wanted a kid brother and I loved following her around as she was guaranteed to get us into trouble! She made me do crazy things right from the time I was 8 or 9 years old - like throwing rocks at me through the window at 3:00 am to wake me up, making me wear my mother's heels to unlock the door so we could have a "midnight picnic". Needless to say we were caught by her dad, my favourite uncle. Not a day went by when we didn't get a smack from our moms because Tina and I were up to some mischief.

As the years went on our bond grew by leaps and bounds. She was my confidante, my best friend, my sister, the first one to know about every crush I had on a girl, and the first one to know when my heart was broken. We had the same friends, the same tastes in music and food and entertainment, we laughed at the same jokes and loved going to the same places for vacations – Nainital was an all time favourite. Once she called me at 1:00 am – "Phunti" as she fondly called me, "lets go to Naini, na". Next morning six of us were on our way at 10:00 am. Only she could convince me to wear her earrings and lipstick and have my picture taken because it was "fun". It was well worth it because her infectious laughter made us all happy. Such was the spirit of fun and adventure in her and she brought out the same in others around her.

Tina grew up to become a beautiful young woman, so vibrant, so full of life and energy. I saw many a boy try to come close to her and even saw a couple of my friends trying to woo her. I was fiercely protective about her and she hated that, although secretly I think she loved the attention. At times I felt she made some wrong choices for friends but she always said I should respect her choices. "Phunti", she would say, "be my friend, not my father". Over time I learned to accept her choices in friends. Of course that never stopped her from deciding which girl was right for me, who I should go out with, and even who would be a suitable wife for me!

As often happens in life, we each became busy with our lives and careers. I left India soon after my CA, got married and settled abroad. She left Delhi in pursuit of her dreams. However, unlike other relationships that grow apart through absence, this made absolutely no difference to us. She was my sister and one doesn't grow apart from one's sister. When we met we had a rollicking good time, just like the good old days. When she moved to the US we would talk on the phone virtually every other day, just like old times, reminiscing about the good old days.

Fast forward a few years, I felt she made some wrong choices in life and deep down I bore a grudge against Tina because I couldn't bear to see my sister go through stress and pain. She was emotionally fragile and I often felt she let people take advantage of her feelings. She never listened and may have paid a heavy price for being a wonderfully caring, loving and gentle person. Today I carry a deep regret for bearing a grudge against Tina for being such a beautiful soul. For a short period of time I had stopped speaking to her, and even though this only lasted a few months, I bear a sense of guilt that perhaps I abandoned my sister when she needed me the most. My other regret is that she never got a chance to really know my son. At their one and only meeting I could see the love in her eyes as she sat him down on her lap and hugged him tightly – it was almost like she sensed she would never see him again.

I can never forget the day when I got the call in Canada that Tina had passed away. I was in the office and still remember my heart sinking as I heard the words from our cousin "Tina has passed away". Those words still echo in my ears. I immediately shut my office door and called her parents, my uncle and aunt. That day I cried. I had not cried since my father's death ten years ago, but that day the tears flowed from my eyes uncontrollably. Today there are just two people who I remember and think of often – my father and my sister Tina. Their pictures hang side by side on the wall at my bedside, both smiling and looking down at me as if to say, "We love you very much, and we are looking out for you".

I miss you very much Tina. You left behind some very happy memories of joyful moments we have shared throughout our lives. You are my angel in the heavens.

Toronto, **Anuj Dhawan**
Canada